Grant Writing Made Simple

87 Tips
for Great Grants

D1715746

Grant Writing Made Simple

87 Tips
for Great Grants

by
Sally Stanton, Ph.D.
and
Laurie Risch, M.A.

CRICKHOLLOW BOOKS

Crickhollow Books is an imprint of Great Lakes Literary, LLC, of Milwaukee, Wisconsin, an independent press working to create books of lasting quality and practical value.

Our titles are available from your favorite bookstore or your favorite library jobber or wholesale vendor.

For a complete catalog of all our titles or to place special orders, visit our website:

www.CrickhollowBooks.com

Grant Writing Made Simple
© 2009, Sally Stanton and Laurie Risch

ISBN-13: 978-1-933987-08-8

First Edition • Original Trade Paperback

Contents

1 **Your Mother Was Right!**   7

2 **Busting the Myths**   9

3 **Tell Me What the Problem Is**   15

4 **Who Are These Grantmakers?**   19

5 **Are We Speaking the Same Language?**   23

6 **Evaluation:**
   What Does Success Look Like?   27

7 **More on Evaluation**   31

8 **Simple but Essential Writing Skills**   35

9 **It's All About Relationships**   39

10 **Picky Stuff that Moms Nag About**   43

11 **It's All About Style, Baby**   47

12 **Courtesy Counts!**   51

13 **Credibility, Confidence, and Modesty**   55

14 **Looking for your Edge**   59

15 **Advice from the Grantmakers**   61

16 **Grant Reviews: The Harsh Reality**   65

17 **Mom Always Has the Last Word!**   69

APPENDICES

Commonly Made Grammar Errors   71

Grantmaker Databases & Directories   73

Recommended Reference Books   75

Glossary of Grant & Nonprofit Terms
        Used in this Book   77

About the Authors   81

Your Mother Was Right!

Faced with a new task, such as learning to write a grant, most people imagine that task to be much more complicated than it actually is. We forget that the simple answer is most often the best. In fact, for many things, our mothers had the right approach: common sense is the main skill, and you will get very far by just doing the basic things well.

Our mothers really were (and still are) right. Even if some of us can admit it only years later!

So we took Mom's pithy comments, advice, admonitions, and warnings on various aspects of life, and applied them to the field of grant writing. We examined our own misconceptions and ah-ha moments while learning and doing grant writing, and thought about what we've said so often to our own kids (and students). This handy little guide is the result.

Grant Writing Made Simple is a quick survival guide and desktop companion for the new grant writer, especially for students studying grant writing while majoring in English, community education, and social work. Along with applying Mom's basic principles, we also picked the brains of grant writing students, foundation grant reviewers, writing instructors, and others, looking for the best and quickest tips and techniques. These little nuggets of wisdom are small enough to fit in your already-crammed-full-of-facts brain, but big enough to help you out when you get stuck at 4:30 a.m. on deadline day.

We've presented the areas where we really think you should put your focus. Grant writing textbooks are chock-full of many great techniques and methods, and we want you to use them, but we're not sure that one size fits all in the grant-writing world, especially when you're trying to learn this skill along with many other responsibilities in your studies or job.

"Learn to walk before you run," Mom said, "Put on one shoe, then the other."

Indeed, long into our professional careers, it turns out that what we most remember and use day to day are the little one-liners that float into our brains when writing, and re-writing, and re-writing that grant narrative for what seems like the 50th time. Your mom may have given you plenty of lengthy lectures on courtesy and cleanliness, but what do you remember?

"Be sure to say please and thank you!"

"Don't run down the stairs; take it one step at a time."

So we've combined the wisdom of moms and grant writers to create this book. Hey, it's always reassuring to know that you can go to Mom for advice, or a reminder, or just a soothing pat on the back and the promise of a chocolate-chip cookie when you finish your assignment. That's what this book is for.

So thank your moms for all they taught you, and enjoy using their sound advice one more time.

Oh, and by the way . . . someday you'll thank us for this.

Chapter 1

Busting the Myths

The process of writing grant proposals can be intimidating, mysterious, confusing, and sometimes downright frustrating. As a result, writers seem to either love it or hate it. And they will passionately describe their experiences and opinions about it!

So you may have heard strong opinions about what works or doesn't work from your friends or colleagues. Despite the stories you may have heard, positive or negative, we recommend that you keep an open mind.

In fact, we personally think grant writing is rewarding and fun, and we hope that you will think so, too.

But before we get into the nuts and bolts of how to go about it successfully, let's do some myth-busting. Let's start by dispelling a few rumors before they become "facts."

Myth 1

"A grant is easy to write—just fill in a few blanks, cut and paste a few paragraphs, and put it in the mail."

Myth Busted: All grant proposals are different. Yes, a few may merely require factual, formulaic information. But most require you to customize a description of an organization and its program. You will need to justify its purpose, assemble supplementary materials, and complete some related tasks. Some proposals may be written in just a few hours, while others might require 40 hours or more. The main thing to remember: Every grantmaker is different. So you'll need to adapt your proposal for each one. Allow more time than you think you could possibly need, to give yourself an ample schedule to put together the best custom batch of answers, materials, and supporting stuff.

Myth 2

"Grants are hard to write. It's impossible to fit so much detail into just a few words, and half the time you don't really know what to write!"

Myth Busted: Like most activities requiring research, knowledge, and focused concentration, grants are really only as hard to write as YOU make them. This book will teach you a few tricks to help you understand what grantmakers want to see in a grant application. By brushing up your English skills, you can learn to write directly, clearly, and concisely. By planning the grant-writing process carefully, conducting thorough information research and analysis, and learning to think from multiple perspectives, not only you can you get through the process of writing a grant, you can actually enjoy it!

> "The one thing I've kept in mind is that being a grant writer is like being a treasure hunter. Not all the clues appear right away, and you need to keep digging, searching, and interpreting until you can even make sense of those clues. If all the facts were already laid out nicely and neatly, our

organizations wouldn't need us in the first place! Much of this process is to find the gold mine that the organizations can't even see . . . and to share the wealth of that treasure with our funding source."

—Michael Cotey, student grant writer, 2007

Myth 3

"Anyone, including individuals and businesses, can apply for a grant."

Myth Busted: Only a small number of programs offer grants directly to individuals and businesses. Most granting programs require the involvement of a nonprofit organization to ensure the funds are used properly and for the public good.

The few grants available directly to for-profit businesses or individuals are very competitive and very specific about eligibility (grantees must be a landscape photographer of Martian descent* who documents the change of seasons in Northwestern Vermont, for example). In fact, the vast majority of grants are intended for nonprofits, which have public-service requirements, are legally accountable to a board of directors, and make their activities (and records) available to the public (that's you and me!).

*just kidding about this part.

Myth 4

"Grant writers create a standard "boilerplate" (see glossary) proposal or letter and send the exact same thing to many different grantmakers."

Myth Busted: A little bit of a boilerplate approach can

help, but it's not the whole answer. Yes, many novice grant writers use a boilerplate, but few achieve success with such an uncritical approach. Carefully researching and selecting appropriate grantmakers will make it clear that each potential sponsor, whether a foundation, a government agency, or a corporate giving program, has its own personality and criteria—its values, interests, and mission.

And it doesn't work to send the same thing to everyone. Most grantmakers have different and often very specific requirements for grant applicants. Choosing the right grantmakers carefully, in order to maximize your potential for success—winning a grant—is smart.

Tailor your proposal to make your case clear. Why should THIS grantmaker give money to THIS organization for THIS program? That's even smarter. This isn't the time for shotgun target practice. Aim directly for the bulls-eye.

By the way, everyone cuts and pastes text between proposals these days, but thoughtful customization for each proposal is absolutely essential. And beware! When re-using text, take care that you change names and other key words or phrases between documents! Proofread carefully. If ABC Foundation receives a letter referring to the XYZ Foundation, your chance of success just dropped to zero.

Myth 5

"Writing grants is like writing school assignments. Finish one, turn it in, and go on to the next."

Myth Busted: Ah, for the good old days when tasks could be gleefully crossed off the to-do list and happily forgotten. You won't be far into the grant-writing process before you learn that successful grant writers must be organized, detail-oriented multi-taskers. Task A might be only half done when you must start working on Task B. Tasks C, D, and E might go down in order like little dominoes, while Task F will work in tandem with the second half of Task A and the middle third of Task B.

This might be a good time to start writing your to-do lists in pencil, as clearly the anonymous writer quoted below must have done:

> "Grant writing [is] a stop-and-go process. One can't get everything done in a day, a week, or a month for that matter... A lot of my work has been slowly inching my way closer to completely grasping what it is I should accomplish."

"Did you finish *ALL* your homework? Haven't you started that report that's due next week? Do you even know what it's supposed to be about?"

Chapter 2

Tell Me What the Problem Is

Obviously, you're writing a grant because a *NEED* exists. (You're thinking, "Yeah, I'm doing this because I need money.") But the main point is that the nonprofit you are working with needs money.

Guess what? This isn't news. Everyone needs money. The secret to getting your grant writing project started is to be absolutely clear to explain what the money is *FOR*.

What problem can be solved, or at least partially solved, with this money?

What need (food, education, etc.) will be satisfied by the program created or funded with this money? What needs to change in your neighborhood, community, country, or world?

Nonprofits are not around to make money for stockholders by convincing people to buy stuff. They exist, instead, to solve problems and fill needs—social, environmental, medical, etc.

Once you figure out what the money is needed for, you should compose a "need statement" (also called a problem statement or case statement). You will use this statement later when you begin writing letters of intent and proposal narratives. A need statement is a concise statement (no more than one page!) of the problem your program solves.

Write it so that it is very clear to the reader that you know what you are talking about. Be specific. Do your research.

Read what others have written about this problem. Get the statistics. Interview everyone. You must understand this problem as well as your nonprofit does—and from its point of view. Ask lots of questions of key people in the nonprofit organization, and ask others involved in that field.

Then start thinking about how you would explain it to your mom. Don't worry about using lots of fancy persuasive language here. Allow the facts to be persuasive. Arrange them so your mom can follow your logic and reach the conclusion you want her to reach.

"You can have your $50, dear . . . if you'll just explain exactly why you need it."

Need Statement Tips

1 The need statement should be focused as much as possible on providing clear information about what must be changed, why it's important to change it now, and how it will be changed.

2 The "what" in No. 1 could be people, the environment, the economy, or anything that affects our lives.

3 The "why" tells your reader what's important about this program or project. Why is change needed? Why now?

4 The "how" describes the activities of the organization and connects them directly to the change desired.

5 Avoid overstating the need. You want to look competent, and you want to convince the grantmaker that the grant will make you more competent, not that you are scrambling for money to keep your program alive. As in dating, desperation is not attractive.

6 If it doesn't already have one, immediately give a memorable name to the program you are hoping to fund to fill the need. (Even if it changes later, you need something to work with to get started. You can't call it program XYZ forever.)

Chapter 3

Who Are These Grantmakers (and What Do They Want from Me)?

Most grant-giving entities (known as grantmakers, funders, or sponsors) publish grant application guidelines. Sometimes they publish something called Requests for Proposals (RFPs), which are usually more specific requests to fill some need that they want to see addressed.

You can find these guidelines and RFPs mostly on the Web these days, although print copies can often still be obtained upon request.

Think of writing a grant as similar to entering a contest. You need to take certain steps to prepare and send in your entry so it will be considered (and not thrown out because some detail wasn't filled out correctly).

Guidelines and RFPs usually give you a step-by-step description of the desired content and the order of presentation for each section of a proposal.

In addition, if you learn to read between the lines, you can discover what a grantmaker values and what problems it is interested in solving. For example, if the guidelines tell you to "be concise, print on recycled paper only, and please don't include supporting documents that are not specifically requested," what does that tell you about the grantmaker?

As a grant writer, you need to be part detective, part psychologist. Get smart.

Read RFPs and guidelines carefully. Then read them again.

Highlight important points. Keep the guidelines handy so you can reread them often.

Make a checklist (if one is not provided) of all the information to be included in the letter or proposal and in what order.

Make another checklist of all the pieces of paper which must be included in the final proposal package.

As you are writing, and later, assembling your grant, make sure you follow all the instructions and rules exactly, or your "contest entry" will be eliminated.

Tips for Working Well with Grantmakers

7 Funding "guidelines" are not just guidelines. They actually are the rules of the game! Adhere to them religiously.

8 Learn the "jargon" or "lingo" of philanthropy. Each grantmaker tries to say the same thing in a different way in its Request for Proposals (RFP) or funding guidelines. Learn which terms and phrases are synonymous, like "need statement," "problem statement," and "case for support."

9 Don't assume. If you don't understand the guidelines, call the grantmaker and ask. It's also a great way to begin a relationship!

10 The wording in guidelines/RFP's can be repetitious. If the same information is requested in two sections, include it in both places. But try to vary your word choices and phrasing, at least a bit, so it does not appear to be a cut-and-paste answer. Within the structure provided, grant writers must stretch their creative muscles.

11 Carefully study grantmaker Web sites for additional clues to understand values, mission, and direction. Keep in mind, however, that Web sites may not always be kept updated. Use common sense to evaluate the credibility of the information.

"Don't believe everything you read, sweetie!"

12 Research the programs your targeted grantmaker has supported in recent years. If possible, review the list and some details of actual proposals that won past grants—especially any for programs similar to yours, or made to organizations of your size, or for similar-sized grant amounts—to discover how to strengthen your own writing.

Sometimes, on grantmaker websites, you can find an actual complete proposal posted. This is a great resource for studying what worked.

In other cases, an employer or client will give the grant writer a copy of a past successfully funded proposal, to review and to borrow from liberally.

Not surprisingly, you'll find that some poorly written grants do get funded. That's because the program rocks.

Still, the combination of a terrific program and a great grant writer is hard to beat.

Chapter 4

Are We Speaking the Same Language?

The whole point of writing a proposal is to create a relationship between a grantmaker. It has money and wants to give it to people who will use it wisely for a good cause. You represent an organization that needs money and wants to use it wisely for a good cause.

What's the best way to encourage this bond? Like running a dating service, or at least hooking up two of your friends, you must convince at least one of them, and ultimately, both, that they have common interests, values, and goals, and that getting together would be great for both of them. Analyze the characteristics of both parties that make this a good match.

Let's say your organization (or you, the grant writer) has done the research and believes a specific grantmaker is Mr. or Ms. Right. Your job is to create the communication piece (the proposal) that will get attention and make the grantmaker in turn feel that perhaps your particular organization is also its Mr. or Ms. Right.

What makes people feel this way?

It turns out it's a lot like successful dating. Speak their language. Present what you're doing in terms that make sense to them. Make them feel understood. Help your prospective grantmaker feel that by "getting together" (giving a grant), it can get what it wants out of the relationship (mission fulfillment).

Let's be honest, most relationships start out by being about what *WE* want, not what the other party wants. You already know what *YOU* want. So stop to think, what do *THEY* want? Focus on learning all you can about that.

Then compare what you both of you want and how well that matches. If the chemistry just isn't there, move on and keep looking for another match.

Tips for Good Communication

13 Every family, organization, and field of study has its own language (known as "jargon")—terms, abbreviations, and acronyms that have a specific definition within that context. Do not assume that funding sponsors will understand your language!

14 Study the grantmaker's guidelines and Web site to identify keywords that will identify "hot buttons" to hit in your proposal. This will help you in both research and writing.

15 Be careful! Do "match" the language, but not to a point where the grantmaker feels you just parroted back its own words. Get a thesaurus and use it. Learn how many ways you can creatively say the same thing.

16 Sometime you do need to use uncommon, unique terms specific to your field, organization, or program. If you do, clearly define all acronyms, industry terms, catchphrases, abbreviations, and program nicknames the first time you use them in a sentence. If the term doesn't appear again for a page or two, re-define them briefly on next use.

17 Ensure accuracy and consistency in use of special terms by creating a custom spell-check dictionary in your word-processing program that includes everything listed in tips #14 and #16.

18 If you are struggling to find commonalities between your proposed program and the grantmaker's guidelines, re-think whether this grantmaker is a good choice. Better to not write a proposal than to write one that is such a stretch that the reader laughs as she tosses it in the "to be shredded" pile.

Chapter 5

Evaluation: What Does Success Look Like?

Program developers use terms like goals and objectives to help everyone understand just what their program is intended to do. However, just as language can change from setting to setting, so can the definitions of seemingly familiar words such as *goals, objectives,* and *outcomes.*

For instance, the word *goal* may have a particular meaning for you in your personal life or in your job, but in grant writing and program evaluation, *goal* has a specific meaning.

We've defined the most commonly used terms in the tips below. You need to know these well before you write your evaluation plan.

In grant-writing jargon, a goal is something bigger, while an objective is a specific, smaller part of that.

To understand how these terms relate to one another, imagine that your goal is to boil water. Your objective is to apply heat to the water, a specific step, and to keep it heating until it reaches 212 degrees.

Two other useful terms: outcome and indicators. The intended outcome is that the water is heated to 212 (it boils). Indicators of a successful outcome include observations of bubbles rapidly rising to the surface of the water, steam rising into the air or collecting in the pot lid, and a thermometer reading of 212 degrees.

Of course, significant problems, like those addressed by most grants, have goals that are more complex. It may have a clear goal, like teaching reading skills to low-income English language learners to improve their employment opportunities. Your objectives might be a list of specific parts of that goal: reaching the right people to serve, convincing them to participate, enrolling them, developing curriculum materials, graduating them.

Your outcome, then, would be some specific measurable change in that target population's reading skills and employment.

What might be some indicators showing that a measure of success was achieved?

(For more about these definitions of key terms, see the examples below in the tips section.)

The evaluation section of a proposal sets out clearly the organization's roadmap for evaluating the success of a project or program. It answers the reader's question, "What does success look like?" with specific, measurable, achievable, realistic, and time-sensitive (SMART) guidelines for assessment. How will you collect data about the indicators, outcomes, objectives completed, and goals achieved?

This is a very important part of the grant, because it allows the granting agency to see that you have thought clearly about how to have a real and measurable impact on some area of need that they agree is important.

Evaluation Lingo

19 Goals are broad statements that describe how your proposed program or project will change people's lives, the economy, the environment, etc. Example: XYZ program will improve children's health in our community by educating parents about proper nutrition.

20 Objectives are specific actions your program will take to achieve your goals. In other words, by fulfilling your objectives, you will reach your goals. Example: XYZ program will offer a free public workshop on five different dates throughout the year and provide up to three in-home visits by a nutritionist for families who attend the workshop. Objectives should contain specific numbers: 100 families will attend the workshops. 85 families will participate in the in-home nutritionist visits.

21 Tasks are the step-by-step actions you take to accomplish your objectives. Example: Survey and interview parents to assess their knowledge of proper nutrition. Design a workshop to fill in the gaps. Select and hire a qualified nutritionist to make home visits. (And so on, usually given in the order in which they will happen.)

22 A Work Plan (also called Method or Methodology and often combined with a Timeline) takes things to another level of specificity.

It is a detailed chart or table that shows what must be done (tasks), when it will be done (timeline), who is responsible for doing it (personnel), and any other information that summarizes sequentially (often chronologically) the process of implementing the program from start to finish. All the tasks together, listed in sequential order, make up the methodology.

23 Outcomes are measurable changes or improvements experienced by program/project beneficiaries. Example: Parents' knowledge of child nutrition improves.

24 Indicators are the concrete, observable evidence that an outcome has been achieved. Example: A comparison of before-and-after parent interviews and one-week food logs shows 90% of parents making more nutritious food choices more frequently.

Chapter 6

More on Evaluation (It's That Important!)

Picture this. You are sitting across from the boss at your yearly performance review. "How do you think you did this year?" she asks. "Convince me that your salary was well spent."

"Er . . . hmm . . .was I supposed to keep a record of what I did?" you mumble.

You scratch your head. "So, did you want charts and stuff?"

Ludicrous, right? Yet many grant writers seem to have the same cavalier attitude toward grantmaker expectations. Maybe you think it can be thought out later; aren't evaluations written when the program is over? Why talk about that at the beginning? How are we supposed to know what to write now? Can't the sponsor just trust us to follow through with our program?

Foundations want and need to know that the money they have entrusted to a nonprofit has been used wisely and for the earmarked purpose. Yes, setting up an evaluation process can be difficult and time-consuming. And yes, that part of the application comes just when time is in short supply.

But the extra effort at this stage may be the difference between receiving a check and receiving a rejection. Don't tempt fate; evaluate!

More Evaluation Tips

25 Evaluation is the step grantmakers most want to see, yet many grant writers skip it entirely, or merely pay it lip service. Therefore, write a well-written, detailed evaluation section that sets your proposal apart from your competition.

26 Grantmakers want to know their money will be spent on the purpose for which it was given. Their grant is an investment in your program. Show them how well you will invest their money by providing a clear plan for monitoring progress and measuring success.

"Money doesn't grow on trees, you know."

27 Design the project evaluation before writing any proposals. If you aren't in charge of the project, insist that the program staff (from the organization you are writing the grant for) work with you to create an evaluation process that is realistic and will satisfy grantmaker requirements.

28 Once the grant is award, and as the program happens, collect evidence of program success (in other words, evaluate) as the activities occur. Don't wait until after the program ends. Ongoing evaluation should be "built into" (meaning it's easy to do) the project as much as is possible and practical for the organization. (And in your application, show grantmakers that you consider evaluation to be part of everyone's job.)

29 Avoid vague or flowery claims. Provide actual data that relates to your goals and objectives. For example, instead of writing passionately, "Our program was hugely successful last year! Everyone loved it!" describe the evidence of your success – "All 150 member families participated in XYZ regularly and enthusiastically this year. On exit questionnaires, every family reported a satisfaction level of 4 or above on a 5-point scale."

30 Include a simple plan for gathering baseline (often called benchmark) data before the program starts. You must have a starting point for comparison, so that you can see if your program made a difference. For example, if your grant seeks to lower blood pressure for a given constituency, include a plan to measure blood pressure or administer a survey before the program activities start.

Chapter 7

Simple but Essential Writing Skills

Writing in the business world (and that includes non-profits!) is very different from the academic writing learned in school. Nonprofits may not make actual profits, but they still carry out business every day (we think it's very important business).

Grantmakers are also carrying out a type of business, and they are not interested in your personal opinion, nor do they want a dry recitation of statistics. They want to know what it is that you want them to do, or perhaps know, and why they should care.

Similarly, when you communicate with others in the nonprofit world during your grant writing project, you are communicating with very busy, working people who want you to do nothing more than get to the point and tell them what you want from them, and why it's important for them to care, and therefore, to act now.

Whether you are writing a letter, email, text message, or grant proposal, it helps to take the point of view that *YOU* are insignificant (but your mom still loves you!). Professional communicators accomplish their goal when their writing is *READER*-centered, not writer-centered.

It's really very simple. Picture the person to whom you are writing. Think about what they know or don't know. How can you make your message so clear that they get it on the first read? How can you avoid wasting their time and yours? Make sure you really understand what you are writing about and why and to whom you are writing.

Mom's All-Purpose Rule of Good Writing: Keep the Reader In Mind, or RIM. Don't assume reader knows the subject as well as you – or knows it at all.

RIM ("Reader in Mind") Tips

31 Learn the basics of business writing, which differ from what you may have learned in school, or what you may be imitating in your workplace. Whether you are writing a one-paragraph email or a 20-page proposal, remember these three critical steps for all writing:

- Understand thoroughly the purpose of your communication.
- Know well your audience and their priorities.
- Revise, revise again, and revise once more!

32 Apply the characteristics of good business writing to your email exchanges and other communications with staff, volunteers, grantmakers, and collaborators: clarity, conciseness, visual appeal, accuracy, and courtesy. If you don't know what these involve, Mom wants you to please read a good business writing textbook or take a business writing course.

33 Read a good email etiquette book (see Appendix for our recommendations). Some practices you think are fine for normal emails between friends and social acquaintances may not be acceptable at all. Remember everything you send electronically may also be forwarded to others, to people who may be future colleagues, employees, partners, or bosses. (Or maybe your Mom!)

34 Choose the right communication method for your audience and your purpose. Determine quickly if the client/grantmaker/boss prefers email, telephone, paper, in-person meetings, etc. Their preference, not yours, rules.

35 Handle complicated matters through voice communications, since most people have short attention spans when reading, and afterward, follow up with a written summary confirming your discussion.

36 Document (record or save a copy of) everything—emails, phone calls, meetings, text messages, etc.—in case of misunderstanding or disagreement.

37 Keep your collaborators frequently updated (at least weekly) on the progress of your work. "Virtual" does not mean "invisible." (Use the phone; no texting!)

Chapter 8

It's All About Relationships

Relationships? You're not looking for a relationship; you're looking for a grant. True. But as a grant writer, you are creating relationships. And just as personal relationships must be thoughtfully nurtured if they are to last, so it will be with grant-maker collaborations.

If building and managing business relationships is uncharted territory for you, don't stress over it. We were all fledglings once. You cannot go wrong if you remember that business affairs really have the same goal as affairs of the heart: your partner's best interests must take priority over your own.

This means that to succeed, get to know potential grant-makers well. It may take a bit of time, but eventually you want to show them why it would be better to team up with your organization than with others who are soliciting grants. Like dating, some relationships start as friendships, as you exchange information, tell each other what you're doing, and look for things to do together that are low in commitment.

Don't lose heart if your first proposals meet with a cold shoulder.

And yes, you may have to kiss a few frogs along the way, but eventually you will find the prince or princess. (No extra charge, by the way, for the subliminal dating advice here.)

Relationship Tips

38 This is a business deal between you and your desired sweetie (uh, grantmaker). Grant seekers must show how the grantmaker will benefit from their proposal.

39 The grantmaker's idea of a quick response to a request for guidelines may not be the same as yours. It can take weeks to receive this information. If you don't have that kind of time, you may need to consider approaching a different grantmaker.

40 Remember that many foundations are small and/or family run. Often the person in charge of grants has another full-time job within the foundation or business. Don't overwhelm the foundation with long emails and lists of questions, and be patient while waiting for responses.

41 Gratitude and humility are excellent relationship-builders. Thank people consistently and often for the smallest contributions. Take responsibility for misunderstandings and conflicts. Offer win-win solutions.

"Did you remember to say thank you?"

42 Always confirm meetings in advance. Take the address, directions, and phone number (which you have also confirmed are correct!) with you if it's your first time on site.

43 Never write or say anything negative about another nonprofit or sponsor. It's not professional and you never know who knows whom. Every town is a small town.

Chapter 9

Picky Stuff that Moms Nag About

Few people lose all concept of time and achieve a trance-like state while paging breathlessly through musty grammar books (and those of us who do, rarely admit it). So we understand why you may balk at learning the difference between a comma and a colon, whine about your spelling issues being a genetic thing, and try to get away with dangling or misplacing a few modifiers here and there.

We understand. But that's no excuse. You still have to submit an error-free proposal (remember all that competition out there?). Believe us, your mother was right—sloppiness is a deal breaker.

Below, we've listed some of our favorite tips for improvement in these areas. Because we are picky English teachers, we've also listed a bunch more in Appendix A, and some great resources in Appendix B. (If we could really have our way, this chapter would take up at least half the book.)

A poorly written proposal starts you off on the wrong foot. It's the equivalent of going on a date with spinach stuck in your teeth.

"Picky Stuff" Tips

44 Print your document, then read it out loud several times to check for misspelled or mistyped words. For example, *their* for *there*, or *to* for *too*. Make corrections, then use your computer's spell-check function.

45 A little bit of time passing helps immensely in proofing. Put the document aside for 24 hours, then proofread it again.

46 Ask someone else to read it for grammar and such. It helps to have another reader, with a fresh set of eyes, check for that last small error you still may have missed. It's worth it. Misspellings look sloppy and reduce the credibility of your organization. Remember, grantmakers are looking for a reason to eliminate you (even subliminally!)

47 Double- and triple-check the spelling of all names—of each and every organization, grantmaker, and individual mentioned. Take the same care with job titles. Demonstrate that your organization is detail-oriented and takes the time to get it right.

48 Do not rely on your word-processing program's grammar check function for 100% accuracy. The warnings are helpful, but sometimes the suggested grammar fixes are wrong for the context (or just plain wrong).

49 Know (or look up) the rules of capitalization. Double-check even the words you think you know well.

50 Use commas appropriately. If you do not know how, learn. Learn it now! (See Appendix for simple rules of comma use). Strive for clarity of meaning.

51 Show what you write to your Mom and see if she gets it. Or show it to any other non-involved person. Is your proposal clear, or is some phrase baffling?

52 Use apostrophes accurately. Please. This makes us crazy! Punctuation of posses-sives vs. plurals seems to be difficult for everyone. Example: "The *grantmakers* are meeting us at noon, not the *grantmaker's* are meeting us at noon." Learn the rules and use them consistently. (*Its* vs. *It's* is a special case—look it up in a good grammar handbook and memorize it!)

"If you aren't sure, look it up!"

Chapter 10

It's All About Style, Baby

Think a little about the style in which you've written the proposal. Is it professional? Confident? Clear?

Or is it chatty? Friendly? Colloquial, with slang and incomplete sentences?

For instance, we've written this book in the friendly, colloquial style. That's because our audience is you, the beleaguered beginning grant writer, who needs all the encouragement you can get.

We wouldn't use this style in writing a grant proposal. No way!

Style matters. To help you think about this, here are three imaginary examples of grant application requesting grants for the (fictional) Clothing for Kids program.

We are sure you will understand why all three were rejected.

1. Submitted by E. Hemingway

The bus stopped in front of the school and all the kids got out and went in. It was a nice school and the teachers were very friendly, and their classrooms were each good, large rooms.

The children went into the cloakroom and put their coats on the hooks. One of the children said to the teacher, "I don't have a coat."

The teacher nodded and went to the blackboard and wrote math problems for the children to solve, and they opened their notebooks and solved them.

2. Submitted by E. Dickinson

Winter is counted coldest
By those who have no coats
To know their bleak discomfort
Please read the grant I wrote.

3. Submitted by C. Dickens

It was the coldest of times, it was the time of global warming, it was the epoch of recession, it was the epoch of windfall oil profits. It was the year of Our Lord two thousand eight. Little Pete had recently attained his two-and-tenth blessed birthday, and it was clearer than crystal that this year, as in the very year last past, there would be no new coat in his gift box.

Okay, you may not be as well known as the unsuccessful grant writers quoted above, but you likely have your own distinctive writing style. Maybe, as you reread your own inspired prose in your grant application, you find yourself sitting with satisfaction and exclaim, "This is gold. Pure gold! I'm sure they'll love my writing style!"

Well, you are going to have to rein in your ego, Shakespeare. Grant writers must set aside their personal styles, communicate in clear, concise language, and focus on the needs of the grantmaker.

It's not about you or your literary ambitions. Really.

"Style, Baby, Style" Tips

53 Keep sentence length to 15-20 words on average. Create interest with sentences of varying lengths. A very short sentence can really make a point. For example, "XYZ requests $5,000 for the ABC program" is much easier to read and understand than this: "We, as a nonprofit that serves thousands of residents, are writing to you today to let you know of an opportunity to contribute to a program that changes lives, the ABC program."

54 Be consistent. Keep the tone and quality of your documents and correspondence as similar to one another as possible.

55 Persuasion should be subtle, not overt. A good program can pretty much sell itself. A grantmaker can tell quickly when you're "fluffing."

56 Don't depend on the passive voice. Use strong, active-voice verbs. (Note, we didn't say: "Strong, active-voice words should be used.") Passive construction dilutes the action and sidesteps saying who will take the action.

57 Avoid overuse of forms of to be (is, are, was, were) and also prepositional phrases and adverbs.

58 Use a variety of descriptive words and phrases to create interest and avoid excessive repetition. For example: "underprivileged families" might also be described as "low-income families" or "households earning less than $_____ per year."

Chapter 11

Courtesy Counts!

A long, long time ago, this section would not have been necessary. Courtesy was a given. People did not carry on boisterous cell phone conversations in the grocery checkout line. Grade schoolers did not punctuate their playground games with four-letter words. No one could tell if little Whitney was wearing her purple thong or the new one with the tiny yellow stars.

Times have changed. The good news: savvy grant writers will use this change to their advantage. Courteous people stand out in the crowd. Maybe you are genetically gifted in this area (or maybe not). If you feel unversed in the ways of old-fashioned courtesy, visit the local library and borrow *Emily Post's The Etiquette Advantage in Business* by Peggy and Peter Post or *How to Gain the Professional Edge: Achieve the Personal and Professional Image You Want* by Susan Morem. (You can probably find cheap used copies online, as well.)

You'll be glad you did. You'll be surprised how good and practical the advice is. (These books are not as stuffy as you might expect; they are actually quite entertaining and eye-opening!)

And then, you will do the courteous thing and write us a thank-you note.

Courtesy Tips

59 You can never go wrong expressing respect and gratitude in a formal document, especially letters of intent. Don't overdo it, though.

60 If your grant proposal is successful, send the grantmaker a thank-you showing how the money was used, such as photos of people involved in funded program activities. This will definitely make your nonprofit stand out from the rest. If you really want to stand out, send a handwritten thank-you. (And write neatly!)

61 However, avoid gifts of any kind. Grant makers naturally are very opposed to receiving anything that hints at being a gift of any value. They don't want any perception of bribery, even in the tiniest way, and they want you to use your organization's resources for program purposes, not for a gift basket.

62 Dress professionally for meetings. You will make a good impression, and as a result, you will feel more confident.

"Are you really going out dressed like that?"

63 Shake hands at the beginning and end of meetings, and thank the grantmaker for the time he/she has given you.

64 Don't overstay your welcome. Take care of business and take your leave.

Oh, yes, and please . . . no gum chewing.

Chapter 12

Credibility, Confidence, and Modesty

Your proposal is competing with hundreds, and perhaps thousands, of other well-written proposals for excellent programs that suggest the perfect solution to the same problem. What will make your proposal stand out? Credibility. You can establish your organization's credibility in multiple ways. To get started thinking about this, ask these questions about the organization:

- What's your track record and what have you learned from past, even from less-than-successful efforts?
- How well do you play with others (target group, community, grantmakers)?
- What are the qualifications of your staff, board, volunteers, and program personnel?

It's not enough to *LOOK* good. Your organization needs to *BE* good at what it does. Your proposal offers an opportunity for you to highlight the strengths of your organization.

Yes, you can brag a little. It's okay to express confidence.

But, please, brag with modesty! And only brag if you can back it up with evidence.

Credibility Tips

65 If awarded a grant, carry out the program, being as faithful to your original proposal as possible. Don't promise anything you can't do! A good rule of thumb (in life as well as grant writing) is to under-promise and over-deliver.

66 If your application is denied funding, let the grantmaker know (communicate!) you are still committed to finding a way to implement your program and that you'll apply again when you have proven your ability to carry it out successfully.

67 Evaluate and document (take photos, attendance, surveys) *ALL* programs. Of course, you want good records of successful ones. It is also a good idea, however, to analyze less successful programs, so that in your next proposal, you can insightfully explain the lessons learned and their impact on your program.

68 When developing the content of your program and the way in which it will be delivered, directly involve the people who benefit in decision-making and planning. Grantmakers want to see evidence of meaningful input from the intended recipients (target population).

69 Develop active partnerships with reputable organizations to expand the reach and quality of your program. Their credibility will help to boost yours. Obtain and include with grants, when appropriate or requested, letters of support from program partners, other grantmakers, and community collaborators.

70 Select program personnel and other staff with solid education, training, and expertise. Highlight their qualifications in your proposal. Especially in the human services and the arts, reputation and talent are critical to successful proposals (and programs!)

Chapter 13

Looking for your Edge

When the grant writing process is going well, it's easy to sit at the computer and start spending the money before the proposal has been mailed. You know your nonprofit's need, you know the grantmaker's mission, and you know how well the two match.

What you don't know is just how many other writers are sitting at their computers making plans to spend those same monies – your grant funds!

Yes, the competition for funding is fierce. The number of nonprofits increases each year, and each year foundations must turn down deserving proposals. If you read the statistics, your high hopes might suddenly be dashed. Relax.

You can find ways to stack the cards in your favor.

What's your edge?

Start thinking about which characteristics give your organization and program an advantage over the competition. What do you do that's more professional, better, different, smarter, more fun, cheaper, or more efficient? (Or maybe all of the above!) Then start thinking about what you can do to communicate your edge to a grantmaker.

"Edge" Tips

71 Remember that small foundations change their priorities every 3–5 years. Deadlines can also change unexpectedly. Stay current.

72 Include testimonials and success stories. Sponsors want to know who has already decided you are good to work with (other sponsors and the target group you serve).

73 Make your reader's job easy. Imagine the grantmaker using a checklist to review your work. Then prepare your proposal so that the checklist information is easy to find.

74 Clearly communicate *WHY YOUR* program/ project really works (or provide the theory and, if possible, the facts that say it will work) and why it's the right time for this solution to the problem.

75 Make your proposal attractive without being fussy. Use bulleted or numbered points, tables, and other graphics to summarize information when appropriate.

76 Submit proposals early and confirm the receipt of the proposal. Imitate the military rule: early is on time, on time is late, and late is unacceptable. Make timeliness part of your edge.

Chapter 14

Advice from the Grantmakers

Ask a group of grantmakers why one proposal stands out from the rest. You will probably get many different answers.

Perhaps Foundation A prefers to put all its gifts to work in a limited geographical area. Foundation B might be attracted to programs that somehow link several pieces of its mission puzzle. Maybe requests that involve collaborations with similar agencies for common causes sail right to the top of Grantmaker C's review pile.

Your research, if it is thorough, will alert you to these sponsor-specific differences.

But what are the generic tips that almost every grantmaker would share with you if given the chance? We contacted foundations we have worked with over the years, and here's what they advise:

Tips from Grantmakers

77 Submit only those proposals that truly fit the sponsor's mission. You may feel your organization's program is one that anyone would find commendable, but asking a sponsor for money to fund a youth music camp when its mission is to clean up local waterways is a waste of everyone's time.

78 If a grantmaker has specific guidelines, follow them! Send sponsors *ALL* the documents they request and *ONLY* the documents they request. Don't just assume you can use a Common Application form for every proposal.

79 Make your proposal as organized as possible. Grant reviewers do not have time to hunt for the information they need. Also avoid sending off-size documents or using outdated technology (like VHS tapes or attachments typed on your ancient computer in WordPerfect.)

80 Include a detailed, realistic project or program budget. Don't ask for a pie-in-the-sky dollar amount. Foundations have closely examined many more grants than you will ever write in your lifetime. They know how much your program should cost. If the request is too high, the foundation will assume you are a sloppy money manager, or worse, dishonest.

"Don't ask for the moon . . . be realistic!"

81 Dramatic appeals will cause sponsors to roll their eyes. On the other hand, a lack of enthusiasm in your writing will pretty much guarantee a lack of enthusiasm in your readers. If you don't care, why should they? Find a middle of the road between too much emotion and too little.

82 Submit your proposal early; late proposals give grant reviewers a bad day! (We're nagging and we know it. Moms are like that.)

Chapter 15

Grant Reviews: The Harsh Reality

This chapter is last for a good reason. If you thought your college instructors were picky about little details, hold on to your hats and say hello to the people who will be reviewing your grant application! These folks put the stick in stickler.

Take the National Institutes of Health (NIH), for example. It uses a scanning tool to check proposal font size. If sections of an application have been photocopied, which makes the print a smidgen smaller than it was originally, the grant is tossed without being read. (No, we are not kidding.)

Grantmakers do this sort of thing for self-preservation. They are flooded with so many requests that there is no time to carefully review them all. So they often start by throwing out all the applications that don't follow the correct instructions. It makes their job easier. (And there's a bit of common sense to it, too; they want to work with competent applicants.

But rather than gritting your teeth and cursing the unfairness of their picky standards, embrace them. Follow the guidelines to a "T" (being certain to make the "T" the correct font size, of course), and your proposal will make it through the hurdles, while the proposals of less conscientious grant writers will be eliminated.

Grant Review Tips

83 Everything must be written exactly according to the sponsor guidelines. Sponsors are overwhelmed with grant requests and are looking for ways to eliminate proposals. For example, don't skip answering a question by stating, "see next page" or "see attached," unless you're directed to do so. Instead, answer the question where they want it answered. Adhere faithfully to space, format, and style guidelines. If they say "No smaller than 10-point font," they mean it.

84 A positive response rate of only 1 in 10 is standard for letters of intent. So 9 in 10 such queries get rejected. Stay upbeat. Writing a grant is like a sales job—rejection comes with the territory.

85 Your competitors (other nonprofits) are looking for every advantage to get the grant. Make sure you find and emphasize *your* advantage(s). Do you have better access to the target population? Do you have more experience than any other organization doing this work? Make sure this edge is clearly stated, and is easy to find, not something hidden in the middle of a long paragraph of other details.

86 Be aware of your weaknesses compared to other, similar organizations. Anticipate grantmaker objections, concerns, or deal breakers— address them openly and show why these "problems" aren't really problems. Recast them in a positive light.

87 We're nagging again. Grantmakers will not listen to your sad story about the flu you had on the weekend. Miss the deadline, you get no review. Set an early deadline for yourself. You'll stand out by submitting the proposal before the published due date.

Chapter 16

Mom Always Has the Last Word!

"If I've told you once, I've told you a thousand times . . ."

Like our moms, we've repeated ourselves on nearly every page and nagged you time and time again throughout this book. That's because we know you need to hear the important stuff over and over, so it sinks into your tiny little . . . never mind.

Mothers nag because they love their children and want the best for them. We want you to excel at grant writing and maybe even enjoy it. Maybe you're buried under a ton of paper and a slew of information, and you can't yet imagine saying "I *LOVE* writing grants!" You really need your mom at a time like this.

"There, there, it will all look better in the morning."

Take a break from your grant writing project now and then. Sometimes a walk, bike ride, or a nap will improve your writing more than continued work will.

Keep in mind your mom's advice when she saw you were getting bored or frustrated with something you were working on: "Why don't you go outside for a while? It's a beautiful day."

Realize that when you are overwhelmed by paper, jargon, style considerations, or writer's block, at some point your proposal will jell, things will fall into place, and you will be amazed at how well you have done.

Don't aim for perfection. The perfect grant proposal will never be written. Aim for excellence!

Avoid negative self-talk ("I'll never get this grant done!"). You *CAN* do this, and you can do it well!

And remember, no matter what, you've always been Mom's favorite!

Commonly Made Grammar Errors

Annoying Grammar and Other Errors
that Grant Reviewers (and Mom!) Want You To Avoid

1. Ignorant comma use (leaving out necessary commas, putting in commas that do not belong)

2. Misuse of irregular verb past participles (especially lie/lay)

3. Sloppy pronoun use (using object pronouns as subject, using subject pronouns as object of preposition, vague or missing pronoun references)

4. Sentence fragments and run-on sentences

5. Incorrect colon and semi-colon use

6. Parentheses (especially when punctuation is involved)

7. Lack of transitions or too few transitions

8. Weak vocabulary

9. Awkward and therefore, confusing, sentence structure

10. Misplaced and dangling modifiers

11. Excessive use of prepositional phrases

12. Too much repetition of vocabulary, sentence structure, etc.

APPENDIX B

Grantmaker Databases & Directories

Foundation Center

Website: http://foundationcenter.org/

Supported by close to 600 foundations, the Foundation Center is a national nonprofit organization, connecting nonprofits and grantmakers with tools they can use. The Center maintains a comprehensive database on U.S. grantmakers and their grants, available to the public through the Center's website and in its five regional centers and national network of more than 400 funding information centers at libraries, nonprofit resource centers, and organizations in every U.S. state. The Center's online subscription database, Foundation Directory Online, provides detailed information about more than 95,000 U.S. foundations and corporate donors and 1.7 million grants; it can be used free on site at all Center locations and Cooperating Collections.

Foundations in Wisconsin

Many states publish their own listings of grantmakers. For instance, in Wisconsin, this guide offers a comprehensive listing of detailed information about Wisconsin-based grantmakers. Includes deadlines, contact information, mission, assets, typical grants awarded, website addresses, and general guidelines. The directory may be purchased in hard copy and is also available online by subscription.

For more information:

Marquette University, Funding Information Center

http://www.marquette.edu/library/fic/

APPENDIX C

Recommended Reference Books

Alred, Gerald J., Charles T. Brusaw and Walter E. Oliu. *The Business Writer's Handbook, 9th edition.* New York: St. Martin's Press, 2008.

Barbato, Joseph. *How to Write Knockout Proposals: What You Must Know (and Say) to Win Funding Every Time.* Medfield: Emerson & Church, 2004.

Barbato, Joseph and Danielle S. Furlich. *Writing for a Good Cause: The Complete Guide to Crafting Proposals and Other Persuasive Pieces for Nonprofits.* Simon & Schuster, 2000.

Barber, Daniel. *Finding Funding: The Comprehensive Guide to Grant Writing.* Bond Street Publishers, 2002.

Brown, Larissa G. and Martin Brown. *Demystifying Grant Seeking: What You REALLY Need to Do to Get Grants.* San Francisco: Jossey-Bass, 2001.

Browning, Dr. Beverly. *Perfect Phrases For Writing Grant Proposals.* New York: McGraw Hill, 2008.

Carlson, Mim. *Winning Grants Step by Step, 3rd edition.* Jossey-Bass, 2008.

Clarke, Cheryl A. *Storytelling for Grantseekers: The Guide to Creative Nonprofit Fundraising.* Jossey-Bass, 2001.

Clarke, Cheryl A. and Susan P. Fox. *Grant Proposal Makeover: Transform Your Request From No to Yes.* San Francisco: John Wiley & Sons, Inc., 2007.

Geever, Jane C. and Patricia McNeil. *The Foundation Center's Guide to Proposal Writing. 5th edition.* Foundation Center, 2007.

Karsh, Ellen, and Arlen Sue Fox. *The Only Grant-Writing Book You'll Ever Need.* New York: Carroll and Graf, 2006.

Miner, Lynn E. and Jeremy T. Miner. *Proposal Planning & Writing. 4th edition.* Westport: Greenwood Press, 2003.

Morem, Susan. *How to Gain the Professional Edge: Achieve the Personal and Professional Image You Want.* New York: Ferguson, 2005.

O'Conner, Patricia T. *Woe is I: The Grammarphobe's Guide to Better English in Plain English.* New York: Riverhead Books, 2003.

Orosz, Joel J. *The Insider's Guide to Grantmaking: How Foundations Find, Fund, and Manage Effective Programs.* Jossey-Bass Publishers, 2000.

Post, Peggy, and Peter Post. *Emily Post's The Etiquette Advantage in Business: Personal Skills for Professional Success.* New York: Harper Resource, 2005.

Robinson, Andy. *Grassroots Grants: An Activist's Guide to Proposal Writing, 2nd edition.* Jossey-Bass, 2004.

Sabin, William A. *The Gregg Reference Manual, 10th edition.* New York: McGraw-Hill, 2005.

Shipley, David and Will Schwalbe. *Send: Why People Email So Badly and What To Do About It.* New York: Alfred A. Knopf, 2007.

Smith, Nancy Burke and Gabriel E. Works. *The Complete Book of Grant Writing: Learn to Write Grants Like a Professional.* Naperville: Sourcebooks, Inc., 2006.

Glossary of Grant & Nonprofit Terms
Used in this Book

B

Boilerplate   A standardized letter or other document used to submit proposals to multiple grantmakers for the same purpose.

C

Capital request or capital funding   A request for funds to be used for construction, equipment, or endowment.

Common application   A standardized grant format used in a given municipality, region, or state.

D

Decline, denial   A letter sent to you when your grant application is not funded.

E

Evaluation (program)   The process of assessing the success and effectiveness of a project or program in addressing the needs of the target population over time.

G

Goal   Broad statements that describe how your proposed program or project will change people's lives, the economy, the environment, etc. Example: "XYZ program will improve children's health in our community by educating parents about proper nutrition."

Grantmaker   A charitable foundation, government agency, or other entity that awards grant funding to nonprofit organizations for its activities. Also known as a sponsor. (See Sponsor.)

I

Indicators   The concrete, observable evidence that an outcome has been achieved. Example: A comparison of before-and-after parent interviews and one-week food logs shows 90% of parents making more nutritious food choices more frequently.

L

Letter of Intent   A letter, from a nonprofit to a foundation, which states the organization's intention to submit a grant proposal and asks for permission to do so.

M

Methodology   A detailed chart or table (also called a Method or Work Plan and often combined with a Timeline) that shows what must be done (tasks); when it will be done (timeline); who is responsible for doing it (personnel); and any other information that summarizes sequentially (and often chronologically) the process of implementing a program from start to finish. All the tasks together, listed in sequential order, make up the methodology.

N

Need Statement   A concise description of a social or other problem to be solved or a need to be met. The statement also describes the solution to the problem and the resources or actions needed to implement the solution. Also known as a case statement.

O

Objectives   The specific actions your program will take to achieve your goals. In other words, by fulfilling your objectives, you will reach your goals. Example: "XYZ program will offer a free public workshop on five different dates throughout the year and provide up to three in-home visits by a nutritionist for families who attend the workshop." Objectives should contain specific numbers: "100 families will attend the workshops. 85 families will participate in the in-home nutritionist visits."

Outcomes Measurable changes or improvements (gains in knowledge, changes in beliefs, attitudes, or behavior) experienced by program/project beneficiaries. Example: "Parents' knowledge of child nutrition improves."

Outputs Often mistaken for outcomes, outputs are the measurable events, activities, or products of a project or program. Example: "16 workshops presented, 4 parent meetings scheduled, a new building completed."

P

Philanthropy The pursuit of solutions to societal ills through financial or other support to nonprofit organizations and individuals.

R

RFP An acronym meaning "Request for Proposals." Similar to the business term "RFQ" or Request for Quotes. An RFP is a formal written request distributed by a grantmaker providing detailed guidelines for preparing and submitting funding proposals.

S

Sponsor A charitable foundation, government agency, or other entity that awards grant funding to nonprofit organizations for their activities. Also known as a grantmaker or funder.

T

Task The step-by-step actions taken to achieve your objectives. Example: "Survey and interview parents to assess their knowledge of proper nutrition. Design a workshop to fill in the gaps. Select and hire a qualified nutritionist to make home visits." (Etc.)

Timeline A chronology of tasks, or benchmarks, to be reached in implementing a program proposed by a nonprofit.

W

Wisconsin Common Application A standardized grant application form developed by the Donors Forum of Wisconsin to streamline the grant review process in Wisconsin. The form includes questions most frequently found on grant applications, and can be a helpful guide for grant writers. Other states, as well as metropolitan areas, often have their own common grant applications.

Work plan   A detailed chart or table (also called a Method or Methodology and often combined with a Timeline) that shows what must be done (tasks), when it will be done (timeline), who is responsible for doing it (personnel), and any other information that summarizes sequentially (often chronologically) the process of implementing the program from start to finish. All the tasks together, listed in sequential order, make up the methodology.

For terms not found in this glossary, or for additional information about terms used in grant writing and philanthropy, please visit:

http://foundationcenter.org/getstarted/
tutorials/gfr/glossary.html

or

http://www.npgoodpractice.org/CompleteGlossary.aspx

ABOUT THE AUTHORS

Sally Stanton is a lecturer in English at the University of Wisconsin–Milwaukee, where she teaches grant writing and professional communications. She is also an adjunct faculty member at Mount Mary College, where she developed the first fully online grant-writing course for the college's English MA Writing program, and at Carroll University, where she teaches in the communication program.

She is also a freelance consultant, creator and director of The Grant Squad™, a team of select professional writers who collaboratively research and prepare nonprofit grant proposals. Sally is also co-developer of Grants As You Go™ (www.GrantsAsYouGo.com), a custom grant-writing coaching service that combines telephone coaching, an online resource center, and professional draft review and editing to train nonprofit personnel in effective grant writing.

She wrote *Grant Writing Made Simple* with Laurie Risch in response to student requests for an easy-to-read handbook that would build confidence in beginning grant writers working in a consulting role with community nonprofit organizations.

Sally lives in Milwaukee and directs Write Now! Consulting (www.WriteNowConsulting.com), offering research, writing, and editing services for nonprofits, and training, coaching, and mentoring services for staff and freelance grant writers.

Laurie Risch is a Madison, Wisconsin, writer and editor. She has taught composition in public and private secondary schools and is currently working on several children's books, while also serving as a member of The Grant Squad™.